The Stock Exchange in Ireland

by Althea

illustrated by Chris Evans

Published by Dinosaur Publications Ltd, Over, Cambridge, Great Britain
for the Council of The Stock Exchange in Great Britain and Ireland

© text Althea Braithwaite 1983
© illustrations Chris Evans 1983

ISBN 0 85122 403 2

In the past, groups of people met
in Dublin and London coffee houses, and
sometimes decided to put their money together
to buy ships.

They sent the ships around the world
to trade with other countries.

If a ship was successful and made money out of
buying goods and selling them to other countries,
the profits were shared out.
Each person would get a share of the profit
according to the share of the money
he had put towards buying the ship.

Many of these voyages took a long time –
sometimes years – and while the ship was away
some of the merchants might
need their money back to spend
on something else. They would go
to one of the coffee houses to see if
anybody wanted to buy their share of the ship.
Later, other businesses all over the country
were financed in the same way:
mines, factories, canals, and so on.

In 1793 the merchants decided
they needed their own place
to do all the buying and selling
of their shares in these businesses,
so they started The Stock Exchange.

Today the Exchange is still the place
where people who want to buy or
sell stocks and shares can meet.

If someone has some savings or spare money
which she wants to grow, she might ask
a stockbroker to buy shares in a company for her.

This means she has a share
in everything the company owns.
When the company makes a profit
it pays her a share of it, because she owns
some of that too. This is called a dividend.

Later, if she needs her money back –
perhaps to help pay for a new home –
she asks her stockbroker
to sell the shares to someone else.
Her stockbroker will also advise on many other
financial matters, such as tax and insurance.

Many people's savings are used to buy
stocks and shares through The Stock Exchange,
often without the people knowing!
They may belong to a pension fund,
whose money is invested through
The Stock Exchange to make it grow
and so provide pensions for retired people.
Trade Unions invest some of their
members' money on The Stock Exchange.

Lots of people have a life assurance policy
and pay a small sum of money every month.
Together this adds up to a large amount.
Some of that money is invested on The Stock Exchange
and will be used to provide the payments which
the Insurance Company has to make when
people retire or die.

A company may need extra money
to build a new factory or pay for new machines
or maybe to invent new things to sell.
It can get this money by selling new shares
through The Stock Exchange.

The people who buy these shares hope
that the company will become
more profitable and that their shares
will be worth more money.

The Government borrows lots of money
through The Stock Exchange
to build new schools, hospitals and roads
and to help pay for many other things.
People lend their money to the Government
and they are paid interest regularly in return.

The Stock Exchange is run by a Council
voted for by the Members of The Stock Exchange.
The Members all have to obey very strict rules
and regulations so that everybody's savings
are safely looked after.

There are Stock Exchange trading floors
in Belfast, Birmingham, Glasgow, Liverpool
as well as Dublin and London.
They all work closely together
to the same rules.

It is important that all investors have
the same information about the companies
so that nobody has an unfair advantage.

If a company has made large profits or losses,
the price of its shares may change.
This news must be kept secret
until everybody can be told at the same time.
This secret news is sent from The Stock Exchange
by computer to all the trading floors.

When a new company wants to raise
money through The Stock Exchange
the staff at the Exchange
carefully study the company's accounts.
They see what the company is doing
and how it spends its money.

They also find out about the people
who run the company and make sure
they are honest and sensible.

A company whose shares are listed
on The Stock Exchange will have to obey
the rules and regulations which make
sure that it is run properly.

The Stock Exchange Dublin meets
for trading twice a day.
First, the Government Broker calls out
the prices at which he is prepared to
buy and sell government stock for the
Government, and these prices
are recorded on the board.
Then the names of the shares of companies
are read out from the board.
As each share is called, stockbrokers
call out the prices at which
they want to buy or sell.
If a buying broker and a selling broker
agree on a price, a deal is done and
they each write it down.
This price is recorded on the board.

NOMINAL SECURITY PRICE NOMINAL SECURITY PRICE NOMINAL SECURITY PRICE NOMINAL SECURITY PRICE NOMINA
CASTLE BRAND
ABBEY
FITZWILTON
CEMENT ROAD
GLEN ABBEY
GOODBODY
ARNOTT
CLONDALKIN
DUBLIN
HALL
BACON
HARCOURT
CORK GAS
PORT SS
CREAN
HETTON
BARROW
BORD NA
BROOKS
CASHELL
BROWN THOMAS
DWYER
AIB
CPL
CANNOCK

The Stock Exchange London is
a big market place.
The traders are called jobbers
and their market stalls are called pitches.
They try to make a profit by buying shares
and selling them for more money.

Jobbers are buying and selling the same
shares in competition with each other.

It is like a market where lots of stallholders
may sell the same sort of oranges
at slightly different prices.

The stockbrokers are the customers.
They come to the market to buy or sell
shares for the investors.

Before telling a jobber
whether he wants to buy or sell,
the broker will ask the price of the shares.
The jobber gives a buying price and
a selling price.

After asking a number of jobbers, the broker
soon knows where he can buy the shares
for the least money, or sell them for the most.

When the broker has found the best bargain,
he and the jobber both write the details
in their own notebooks. The deal is done.

The actual transfer of the shares
to the new owners is done later in the offices
and then the money will be paid.
Accounting and paperwork
is mostly done by computer
and this makes things much easier.

At the end of each day's trading session
a bell is rung and the market is closed.

The Stock Exchange helps the Government
to borrow the money it needs
to run the country.
Companies can get money
to help them make and sell more goods.
They hope this will increase their profits.
Part of these profits are paid as dividends to the investors.
Some is paid as tax to the Government,
which uses this money to help run the country.
Money left over is kept in the company
to pay for new factories, new machinery,
and the other expenses of running and
developing the business.

People who save money for the future
can invest it and earn extra money.
They also know they can get their savings
back quickly when they need the money.

Glossary

Bear — Someone who thinks prices will go down.

Broker — The Stockbroker (or 'broker') is the person who buys or sells shares for a customer.

Bull — Someone who thinks prices will go up.

Dividend — Part of a company's profit paid to shareholders – usually twice a year.

Interest — Money paid for the use of money borrowed.

Investor — The saver or organisation which buys stocks and shares.

Jobber — A Jobber trades in shares, buying or selling them to brokers.

Pension Fund — A fund into which people put part of their pay. It gives them a pension when they stop working.

Shares	People pay money to the company and in return get a share in the company, so shareholders are the real owners. They hold regular meetings to hear how the company is being run.
Stag	Someone who buys shares in a new company hoping that when they are first resold on The Stock Exchange the price will go up and he will make a profit.
Stocks	Another word for shares, also Government and other loans on which investors receive interest.
Trading Floor	The market place of The Stock Exchange where shares are bought and sold.
Waiter	Someone employed to help on the floor of The Stock Exchange taking messages etc. Called a waiter because long ago, the waiters in the coffee houses used to take messages.

You can arrange to visit your nearest Stock Exchange to see it all working and find out more for yourself.

The Stock Exchange, Dublin